D1736455

SOUTH AMERICA

Go Exploring! Continents and Oceans

By Steffi Cavell-Clarke

©This edition was published in 2018. First published in 2017.

Book Life
King's Lynn
Norfolk PE30 4LS

ISBN: 978-1-78637-044-0

Written by:
Steffi Cavell-Clarke

Edited by:
Grace Jones

Designed by:
Natalie Carr

A catalogue record for this book is available from the British Library.

All facts, statistics, web addresses and URLs in this book were verified as valid and accurate at time of writing. No responsibility for any changes to external websites or references can be accepted by either the author or publisher.

SOUTH AMERICA

CONTENTS

PAGE 4   What Is a Continent?

PAGE 6   Where Is South America?

PAGE 8   Oceans

PAGE 10   Countries

PAGE 12   Weather

PAGE 14   Landscape

PAGE 18   Wildlife

PAGE 20   Settlements

PAGE 22   The Environment

PAGE 23   Glossary

PAGE 24   Index

Words in **red** can be found in the glossary on page 23.

WHAT IS A CONTINENT?

A continent is a very large area of land that covers part of the Earth's surface. There are seven continents in total. There are also five oceans that surround the seven continents.

ARCTIC OCEAN

EUROPE

ASIA

NORTH AMERICA

ATLANTIC OCEAN

AFRICA

SOUTH AMERICA

EQUATOR

INDIAN OCEAN

AUSTRALIA

PACIFIC OCEAN

SOUTHERN OCEAN

ANTARCTICA

The seven continents are home to the Earth's **population.** Each continent has many different types of weather, landscape and wildlife. Let's go exploring!

WHERE IS SOUTH AMERICA?

South America is **located** to the south of North America and to the north of Antarctica. It is mostly surrounded by ocean. To the west is the Pacific Ocean, and the Atlantic Ocean is to the east.

South
America

Pacific
Ocean

Atlantic
Ocean

Amazon River

Population: 414.3 million

A very thin strip of land connects South America to North America. The continent of South American sits on the **Equator**. The Equator runs along the middle of the planet, which is the warmest part of the world. The type of weather near to and on the Equator is very warm and wet.

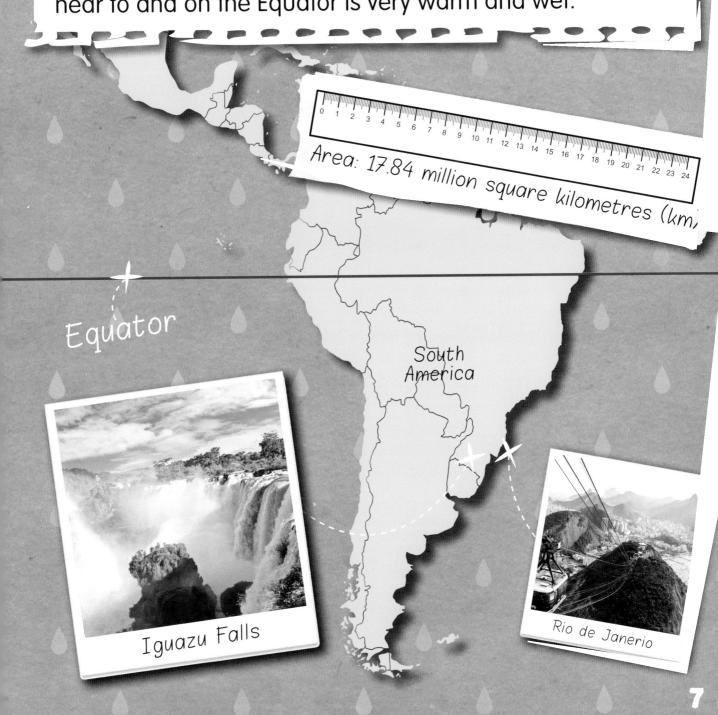

Area: 17.84 million square kilometres (km)

Equator

South America

Iguazu Falls

Rio de Janerio

OCEANS

A sea is an extremely large area of salt water. The biggest seas in the world are called oceans. Just like countries, seas and oceans have different names. South America is mostly surrounded by the Pacific and Atlantic Oceans, and is south of the Caribbean Sea.

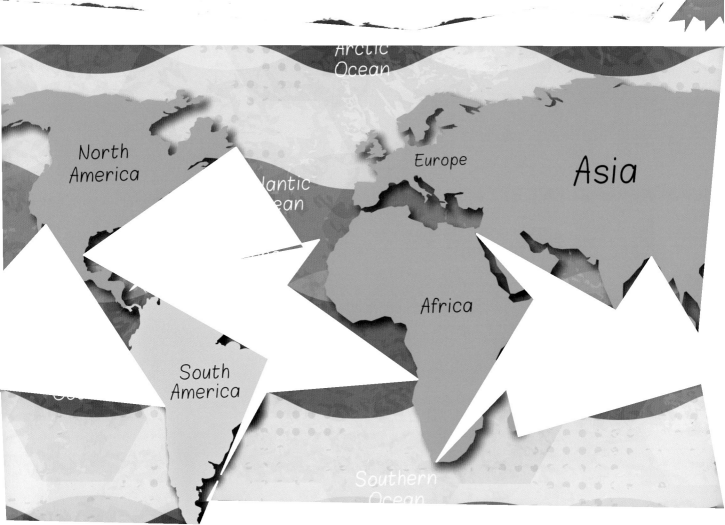

FACT FILE

Atlantic Ocean:
Area: 15% of Earth's surface
Average Depth: 3,339 metres

Pacific Ocean:
Area: 31% of the Earth's surface
Average Depth: 4,280 metres

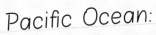

Depth is how deep the water is.

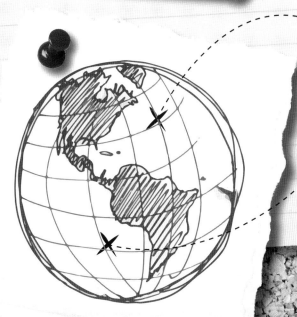

Atlantic Ocean

Pacific Ocean

COUNTRIES

South America has 15 different countries and **territories** in it.

Venezuela

Guyana

Suriname

Colombia

French Guiana

Galápagos Islands

Brazil

Peru

Ecuador

Bolivia

Chile

Paraguay

Argentina

Uruguay

Falkland Islands

FACT FILE

Largest Country	Brazil	Fifth Largest country in the world
Most Populated Country	Brazil	Over 202 million
Famous Landmark	Christ the Redeemer, Brazil	35 metres high
Highest Peak	Aconcagua, Argentina	6,959 metres high
Largest Bird	Andean Condor	3.2 metre wingspan

WEATHER

The **climate** in South America changes across the continent. It has a **tropical** climate in the north, and becomes colder towards the south.

South

North

Places near the Equator get more heat from the Sun, so they have a warm...

The Amazon Rainforest has a warm and wet climate and it rains there almost every day. The warm temperatures and rainfall help the rainforest to grow.

The month of March has the most rainfall every year in the Amazon Rainforest.

LANDSCAPE

There are many different types of landscape across South America. There are rainforests, deserts, **grasslands** and mountains.

The world's longest mountain range stretches along the west coast of the continent, the range is called the Andes.

The Amazon Rainforest is the world's largest rainforest. It covers much of South America. It has thick, green **vegetation** and is home to the Amazon River.

Amazon River

Amazon Rainforest

The Amazon River is over 6,900 metres long.

The South American continent also includes the Galápagos Islands, which are located off the north-west coast of South America in the Pacific Ocean.

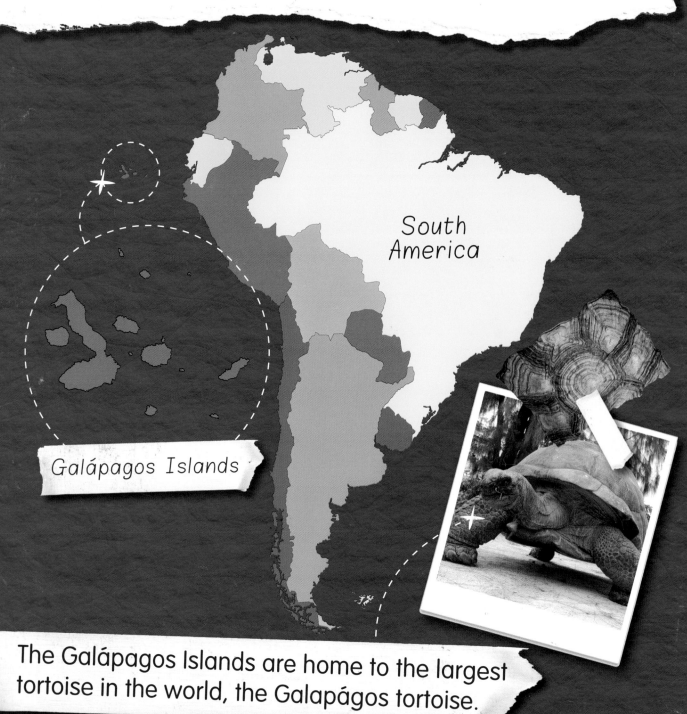

South America

Galápagos Islands

The Galápagos Islands are home to the largest tortoise in the world, the Galapágos tortoise.

Sea Bed

Underneath the surface of the Pacific and Atlantic Oceans, there are sea beds which are covered in sand, mud and rock. The sea bed has an uneven surface just like land.

WILDLIFE

There are many different types of animal life in South America. Wildlife can be found all over the continent.

Sloth

Piranha

Black Panther

Flamingo

Tortoise

Armadillo

Parrot

Crocodile

Darwin Frog

The Amazon rainforest is home to thousands of **species** of animal. The warm and wet climate of the rainforest helps the plants and trees to grow. The trees help to provide food and shelter for animal life.

SETTLEMENTS

Almost half of South America's population lives in Brazil. Lots of people live and work in big cities, such as São Paolo.

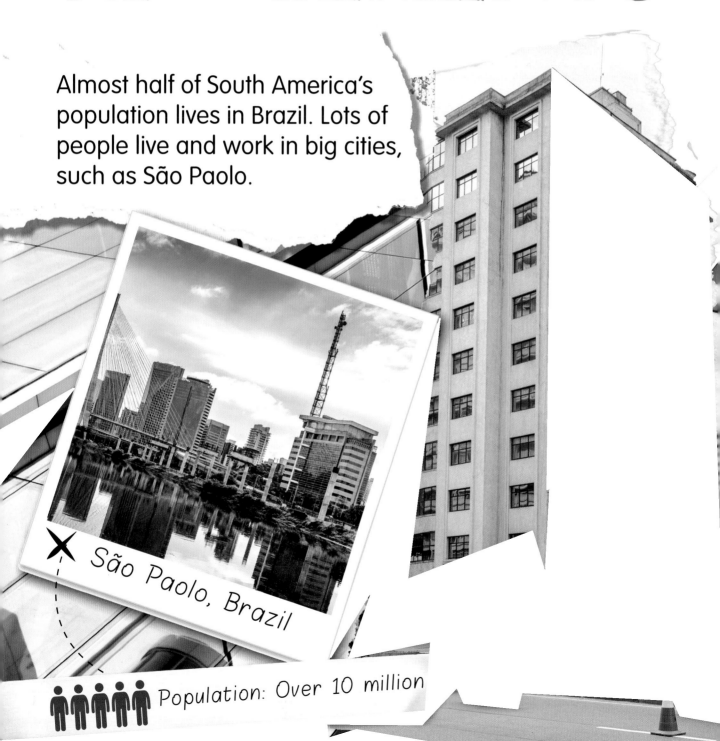

✗ São Paolo, Brazil

Population: Over 10 million

There are many farming villages across South America. Farmers in Brazil grow more sugar cane and coffee beans than almost any other country in the world.

Sugar Cane Farming

Coffee Beans

Coffee Bean Field

THE ENVIRONMENT

Deforestation is a major threat to the Amazon rainforest. Thousands of trees are cut down, which destroys the natural **habitats** of many animals, leaving them without a home. We can help stop deforestation by replanting the trees that are cut down.

GLOSSARY

climate the average weather of an area

deforestation cutting down and removing trees from a forest

Equator imaginary line running around the middle of the earth

grasslands large, flat areas of grassy land

habitats places where plants or animals live

located where something can be found

mountain range a group of connected mountains

population number of people living in a place

species a type of animal

territories areas of land claimed by a country

tropical warm and wet areas near the equator

vegetation types of plant found in an area

INDEX

Amazon rainforest 13, 15, 19, 22
animals 18–19, 22
Atlantic Ocean 4, 6, 8–9, 17
Brazil 10-11, 20-21
Caribbean Sea 8
cities 20
climates 12–13, 19
continents 4–5, 7, 12, 14, 16, 18
deforestation 22
earth 4–5, 9
equator 4, 7, 12
Falkland Islands 10

farming 21
Galápagos Islands 10, 16
islands 10, 16
landscapes 5, 14
North America 4, 6–8
oceans 4, 6, 8–9, 16-17
Pacific Ocean 4, 6, 8–9, 16–17
populations 5–6, 20
rainforests 13–15, 19, 22
seas 8, 17
weather 5, 7, 12
wildlife 5, 18

PHOTOCREDITS